T0120831

LIFE OF PRAYER
A Book of Prayer for All

Mikinson Henry

WESTBOW
PRESS®
A DIVISION OF THOMAS NELSON
& ZONDERVAN

Copyright © 2022 Mikinson Henry.

All rights reserved. No part of this book may be used or reproduced by any means, graphic, electronic, or mechanical, including photocopying, recording, taping or by any information storage retrieval system without the written permission of the author except in the case of brief quotations embodied in critical articles and reviews.

This book is a work of non-fiction. Unless otherwise noted, the author and the publisher make no explicit guarantees as to the accuracy of the information contained in this book and in some cases, names of people and places have been altered to protect their privacy.

WestBow Press books may be ordered through booksellers or by contacting:

WestBow Press
A Division of Thomas Nelson & Zondervan
1663 Liberty Drive
Bloomington, IN 47403
www.westbowpress.com
844-714-3454

Because of the dynamic nature of the Internet, any web addresses or links contained in this book may have changed since publication and may no longer be valid. The views expressed in this work are solely those of the author and do not necessarily reflect the views of the publisher, and the publisher hereby disclaims any responsibility for them.

Any people depicted in stock imagery provided by Getty Images are models, and such images are being used for illustrative purposes only. Certain stock imagery © Getty Images.

Scripture texts marked (NABRE) in this work are taken from the New American Bible, revised edition © 2010, 1991, 1986, 1970 Confraternity of Christian Doctrine, Washington, D.C. and are used by permission of the copyright owner. All Rights Reserved. No part of the New American Bible may be reproduced in any form without permission in writing from the copyright owner.

Scripture quotations marked (NJB) are from The New Jerusalem Bible, copyright© 1985 by Darton, Longman & Todd, Ltd. and Doubleday, a division of Random House, Inc.

Scripture marked (DRA) taken from the Douay-Rheims Bible.

ISBN: 978-1-6642-5422-0 (sc)
ISBN: 978-1-6642-5424-4 (hc)
ISBN: 978-1-6642-5423-7 (e)

Library of Congress Control Number: 2021925682

Print information available on the last page.

WestBow Press rev. date: 05/13/2022

Ecclesiastical Censor: The Reverend Leonardo J. Gajardo, JCL, STD

Ecclesiastical permission: The Most Reverend Robert John
McClory, JD, JCL, DD
Bishop of Gary,
November 22, 2021

Ecclesiastical permission (*licentia*) is an official declaration that a book contains nothing contrary to doctrine, in regard to faith and morals. No implication is contained therein that those who have granted the permission agree with the content, opinions, or statement expressed in this book.

Contents

＊ ＊ ＊ ＊ ＊ ＊

SECTION I 1

Prayers to God the Father

➤ A Prayer to Help Have a Pure Heart 2
➤ A Prayer to Help Be a Good Steward in the Community........ 3
➤ A Prayer to Help Stay in Harmony with God 4
➤ A Prayer to God for Mercy and to
  Help Stay in His Presence.. 5
➤ A Prayer to Help Stay True to God's Teachings 6
➤ A Prayer to Help You Become More Active in God's Plan 7
➤ A Prayer to Help You Carry God's Love in Your Heart 8
➤ A Prayer to Never Worry and Never Compromise
  Your Faith for Something That Is Untrue 9
➤ A Prayer to Help Stay True to God's Law 10
➤ A Prayer to Help Be in God's Spirit 11
➤ A Prayer to Help See God in Every Human Being
  and to Help Love Like Him 12
➤ A Prayer to Never Offend God and Stay True to His Law...... 13
➤ A Prayer to Help Live in Accordance with God's Law 14
➤ A Prayer to Help Do What Is Acceptable to God 15
➤ A Prayer to Help Keep God's Love Burning........................... 16
➤ A Prayer to Help Live in God's Presence.............................. 17

SECTION II 19

Prayers to Jesus for All Needs

- ❯ A Prayer to Help Stay in the Presence of God 20
- ❯ A Prayer to Help Stay in Jesus's Spirit 21
- ❯ A Prayer to Always Be with the Lord in Spirit 22
- ❯ A Prayer to Help Be an Example of Jesus's Laws
  and Teachings 23
- ❯ A Prayer to Jesus When in Danger 24
- ❯ A Prayer to Help Follow God and Resist Temptation 25
- ❯ A Prayer to Help Love God's Creation 26
- ❯ A Prayer to Help Stay in God's Care and Boundaries 27
- ❯ A Prayer to Help Follow Our Savior, Jesus 28
- ❯ A Prayer to Help Stay on Principles and Be in the
  Lord's Presence 29
- ❯ A Prayer to Help Imitate Jesus, the Christ 30
- ❯ A Prayer to Help See God's Love and Follow God 31
- ❯ A Prayer to Help Be an Example of God's Grace 32
- ❯ A Prayer to Our Lord to Keep Safe 33
- ❯ A Prayer to Stay Clean and Stay in God's Spirit 34
- ❯ A Prayer to Help Live in the Lord's Spirit 35
- ❯ A Prayer to Help Resist Temptation 36
- ❯ A Prayer to Help follow God's lead 37
- ❯ A Prayer to Help Live in Accordance with God's Law 38
- ❯ A Prayer to Help Love Others Like God 39

SECTION III 41

Prayers to the Blessed Mother and St. Joseph

- ❯ A Prayer to Help Follow God's Example 42
- ❯ A Prayer to the Holy Mother of God to Help Stay
  in God's Presence 43
- ❯ A Prayer to Help Make the Right Decisions and
  Stay in Harmony with God 44
- ❯ A Prayer to Help be obedient to God's Law 45

➤ A Prayer to Help Stay Focused on our Obligation
and Help Protect Our Loved Ones 46
➤ A Prayer to Help Come Back to the Father, Your
God, and Help Find the Way 47
➤ A Prayer to Help Stay under the Blessed Mother's Care 48
➤ A Prayer to Help Foster Those Who Are under
God's Care and Love 49
➤ A Prayer to St. Joseph to Help Always Show God's
Love to Your Spouse 50

SECTION IV 51
Prayers to the Holy Spirit and the Holy Angels

➤ A Prayer to Help Walk with God and Proclaim
His Love to His Children 52
➤ A Prayer to Help Protect You from Danger 53
➤ A Prayer to Help Protect Children from Abuse 54
➤ A Prayer to Help You Be in God's Presence 55
➤ A Prayer to the Holy Angels to Keep Safe from Danger 56
➤ A Prayer to Stay Steadfast Against the Enemy of God 57
➤ A Prayer to Help Keep You Safe 58

SECTION V 59
Prayers for Special Occasions and Intentions

➤ A Prayer for Success on Your Exams 60
➤ A Prayer to Help Prepare to Meet God in the Next Life 61
➤ A Prayer to God to Help Proclaim the Good News 62
➤ A Prayer for Special Intentions 63
➤ A Prayer before Receiving Holy Communion 64
➤ A Prayer to Help Carry Out God's Mission 65
➤ A Prayer to Keep Safe from Injury while Playing Sports 66
➤ A Prayer before or during Surgery 67

SECTION VI... 69

Prayers for Protection

> A Prayer to Overcome Evil 70
> A Prayer to Help protect from evil doers 72
> A Prayer for God's Protection 73
> A Prayer for Protection and to Always Do What Is
> Pleasing to God...74
> A Prayer to Help Keep Communities Safe 75
> A Prayer to Help Protect Mothers and Unborn Babies 76
> A Prayer for the Protection of Teachers and Evangelizers ... 77
> A Prayer of Protection for Those Who Need Help............... 78
> A Prayer for the Protection of the Pope 79
> A Prayer to God the Father for Protection........................... 80
> A Prayer to Help Protect Children from Danger 81
> A Prayer to Help Protect God's Children 82
> A Prayer to Protect All Mothers 83
> A Prayer to Help Protect the Authorities in a Country 84
> A Prayer for Protection against Evil..................................... 85
> A Prayer for God's protection while asleep 86
> A Prayer to Help Protect the Vulnerable and Stay
> Committed to Help Facilitate God's Work and Mission 87
> A Prayer to Help Protect against Evildoers 88
> A Prayer for God's Protection 89
> A Protection Prayer for Those Who Are
> Ministering Your Church... 90
> A Prayer for the Protection of Schoolchildren......................91
> A Prayer for Protection to Those Who Have Trust
> in the Lord... 92

Acknowledgments

❋ ❋ ❋ ❋ ❋ ❋

Reflective Readers: Bishop Robert J. McClory
Bishop Donald J. Hying (2019)
Bishop Emeritus Dale J. Melczek
Rev. Patrick J. Kalich
Rev. Jerry Schweitzer
Rev. Jeffrey Burton
Rev. Kevin Huber, DMin
Rev. Kevin M. Scalf, CPPS
Rev. Tim McFarland, CPPS
Rev. Leonardo J. Gajardo, JCL, STD
Deacon Daniel Lowery, PhD
Deacon Dennis Guernsey
Deacon Peter Znika Jr.
Deacon Michael Cummings
Deacon Tom Gryzbek
Deacon Martin J. Brown
Barbara Lowery
Anthony M. Bonta, PhD
Pelfrene Saint-Fort
Janet Guernsey
Joseph E. Ware
Mary S. Ware
Bastien Henry
Lannie Cummings
Ingrid Znika
Thomas James

Sandra Henry
Clara Henry
Roseline Pierre Saint-Fort
Merissaint Desliens
Depeigne Henry
Kerline Henry
Tod Linklater
Kerry Linklator
Sr. Barbara Sheehan
Disma Saint-Fort
Paul Rodney Henry
Marie Yvrose Saint-Louis
Witny Henry
Mrs. Marian Weeks
Sr. Sallie Latkovich, SCJ
Sr. Joanne Marie Schutz, SSCM
Kathleen A. Lyons
Bryan Mumaugh
Amy Mumaugh
Maryann Foster
Dave Foster
Tony Sipich
Collette Jeffries
Tommy Lustina
Colleen Lustina
Jen Mucha
Rich Hobby
Maria Gerodemos
Maudeline Bolivar-Henry

Editor and Proofreader: Megan Henry

Preface

* * * * * *

The Holy Spirit dwells in me and inspires me to write prayers. God is using me as an instrument to bring across his prayers and his message. God's love for me helps me be conversant with his message. God helps me follow the path that can lead to something greater than what is on earth. God facilitates me to write these prayers so that they may help you stay focused and obtain a deeper, everlasting relationship with God.

Introduction

* * * * * *

I hope these prayers will be a great source of help for you when you are meditating and praying to our Lord, our God. Also, I hope you will continue to use these prayers to communicate with God and speak in a clearer way to God. Let God's love rain on your dry desert; let God's Spirit dwell inside of you, and let your heart adhere to his love so that, together, we can have one flock, one shepherd, one band, and one orchestra.

Section I
PRAYERS TO GOD THE FATHER

A Prayer to Help Have a Pure Heart

Almighty God, make my heart pure like yours. Make my heart impervious to prejudice, injustice, judging others, unfairness, and hatred.

Help me come to grips and understand that you are the only true living God.

Help me desire nothing but to carry your love inside me and to be able to show it to every one of your creatures.

Amen.

A Prayer to Help Be a Good Steward in the Community

* * * * * *

Dear loving Father, help us grow in your presence as a community of God.

Help us carry your love inside each of us in this community. Help us carry your presence in our hearts, minds, and souls.

Help us be good stewards in our community, always follow your lead, and always be faithful to your Law.

Amen.

A Prayer to Help Stay in Harmony with God

＊ ＊ ＊ ＊ ＊ ＊

Dear God, help me have the right approach in everything I do.

Help me overcome any difficulties that come my way—even when the road seems strenuous and treacherous.

Help me stay and live in harmony with my family, friends, and neighbors.

Help me keep your Law in my heart and carry your love and likeness inside me wherever I go.

Amen.

A Prayer to God for Mercy and to Help Stay in His Presence

* * * * * *

God of mercy, have pity on me. Have pity on your poor child who is in a quandary and does not know where to go.

Help me be in your presence—and help me always see your light around me.

Help me abrogate any erroneous teachings that come to my attention.

Let me live within the boundaries of your Law and your precepts.

Help me escape like a bird from falling into temptation and into darkness.

Let me live within your presence—and let me follow your lead wherever I go.

Amen.

A Prayer to Help Stay True to God's Teachings

* * * * * *

Dear loving God, help me shine like the sun and keep my soul from all the impurity in this world.

Turn my life into "frankincense, myrrh, and gold."[1]

Turn my world into your world and help me be conducive to your church and my community.

Help me always rescind and stay away from erroneous teachings.

Help me approach everything the right way.

Amen.

---

[1] Matthew 2:11 (NABRE).

A Prayer to Help You Become More Active in God's Plan

* * * * * *

Dear Father, help me never abuse my own free will and always stay in the boundaries of your Law and your image.

Help me stay away from all the things that are worthless in my life. Help me be a more active player in your plan and also in my plan "to reach the path of salvation."[2]

Amen.

---

[2] Titus 2:11–12 (NABRE).

A Prayer to Help You Carry God's Love in Your Heart

* * * * * *

Dear God, "you are the Shepherd and I am the sheep."[3] Without you, my life is a mess.

Without you, I do not exist.

Help me see the sacrifice that you made on the cross in order to give us life.

Help me treat others with dignity and respect.

Attach my stony heart onto yours and mold it into the goodness of your presence.

Help me breathe in your Spirit to have the same vision that you have—and help me carry the same love that you carry in your heart.

Help me abide by your Law and be a part of your plan here on earth and in heaven.

Amen.

---

[3] Ezekiel 34:12 (NABRE).

A Prayer to Never Worry and Never Compromise Your Faith for Something That Is Untrue

* * * * * *

Dear loving God, help me see you in every action and every aspect of my life.

Help me stay away from vanities that are destroying your children on earth.

Help me understand the value and the importance of your Law and the meaning of life.

Help me never lose or compromise my faith for something that is untrue.

Help me never get worried about anything—and help me magnify your love.

Amen.

A Prayer to Help Stay True to God's Law

* * * * * *

Almighty Father, you love everything you have created.

Embrace me with your loving care and your tenderness.

Do not let me fall into confusion. Keep me steadfast.

Help me have an unequivocal mind—and help me understand the way of your Kingdom.

Help me stay always sharp and fresh in everything I say and do, each and every day.

Help me stay true to your Law and stay focused under your generous and abundant love.

Amen.

A Prayer to Help Be in God's Spirit

* * * * * *

Dear Father, you showed me how to love by the love that you have given your Son, Jesus Christ.

Help me be in your presence and imitate your loving care as a Father.

Help me be in your Spirit to follow your Law and your precepts.

Help me show that same Spirit to my children and others. Amen.

A Prayer to Help See God in Every Human Being and to Help Love Like Him

* * * * * *

Dear God, your love is like snowfall on a sunny day.

Please! Help me love like you.

Help me see you in every human being you have made with your loving hands.

Help me see your light that is never extinguished.

Make my heart pure like yours—and "clothe my nakedness."[4]

Amen.

---

[4] Matthew 25:36 (NABRE).

A Prayer to Never Offend God and Stay True to His Law

* * * * * *

Almighty and ever-living God, help me know and love you better, as I do the same for my brothers and sisters.

Cling to me as your child once more. Help me do everything according to your will.

Help me never be offensive to you, stay true to your Law, and be always in your presence—now and forever.

Amen.

A Prayer to Help Live in Accordance with God's Law

* * * * * *

Eternal Father, you renew the face of the earth, renew our hearts, and give us new faces and new hearts that are acceptable to you and your Law.

Mold our nature and our spirits into yours—and unify our lives into your life.

Help us live in accordance with your Law, in harmony with your people, and in your presence.

Amen.

A Prayer to Help Do What Is Acceptable to God

* * * * * *

Dear God, everything you have created belongs to you.

Help us sanctify our hearts in the radiance of your love.

Unite us in your Spirit—and help us stay away from evildoers.

Help us to do always what is right and acceptable to you so that we may carry your image and share your love with one another throughout the world.

Amen.

A Prayer to Help Keep God's Love Burning

❋ ❋ ❋ ❋ ❋ ❋

Dear God, help me understand you better.

Help me love you, my neighbors, and others the same way I love you.

Help me see your love in every human being I come across.

Help me desire nothing but good for myself and my fellow citizens.

Help me love like you.

Amen.

A Prayer to Help Live in God's Presence

٭ ٭ ٭ ٭ ٭ ٭

Dear God, "I was hungry, you fed me."[5]

"I was thirsty"[6] for your love, and you showed me the way.

"I was in darkness, and you showed me the light."[7]

I had a stony heart, and you turned it into a sponge.

I had a myopic mind, and you turned it into a bright star.

I was a procrastinator, and you made me a hardworking man.

I was lost, and I found life in you.

Help me always live in you and follow your Law.

Amen.

---

[5] Matthew 25:35 (NABRE).
[6] Matthew 25:25 (NABRE).
[7] Isaiah 58:10 (NABRE).

Section II
PRAYERS TO JESUS FOR ALL NEEDS

A Prayer to Help Stay in
the Presence of God

Teacher, enkindle the love that is in our hearts.

Make our hearts tender when they are surrendered to you.

Help us be in your Spirit.

Help us comprehend the love that you give us because your words are the testimony of our lives, and our lives are the living presence of your love.

Amen.

A Prayer to Help Stay in Jesus's Spirit

❖ ❖ ❖ ❖ ❖ ❖

Jesus, your name means life, love, purity, charity, security, tranquility, faith, hope, kindness, intellect, High Priest, Savior, Caregiver, Lawgiver, Judge, Mediator, Redeemer, rain, snow, chill, thunder, lightning, hail, frost, snow, ice, Rabbi, Servant, Father, Truth, prosperity, and eternity. You are the river that never dries, the light that is never extinguished, the heart that never stops beating, the lungs that are always breathing, and more. You are everything attributed to good and everything that came into being. If I continually write who you truly are in this paragraph, I will run out of space—even if I had an astronomical number of blank pages.

Let me live and die in your arms. Make my heart clean and pure like yours.

If I can sum it up in five words, I can say that you are "the Alpha and the Omega."[8]

Amen.

---

[8] Revelation 22:13 (NABRE).

A Prayer to Always Be with the Lord in Spirit

* * * * * *

Lord Jesus, without your love, I am not alive.

You have shown your love for me by dying on the cross, and that is sufficient for me to seek the truth and nothing but the truth.

You have never let me down when I needed you.

Please keep me at your side always—and help me always have your Spirit in everything I am involved in.

Give me the means and the abilities to always be on the side of those who are in need of your care, your love, and your helping hands.

Help me help those who cannot take care of themselves and always have your love attached to my heart.

Amen.

A Prayer to Help Be an Example of Jesus's Laws and Teachings

* * * * * *

Jesus, you are "the Shepherd and I am your sheep."[9]

"Please keep me in your flock, never let me stray from you."[10]

Give me strength and courage to continue my journey and follow the path that leads me to you.

Make my heart pure and clean like yours.

Elevate my spirit into yours—and let others see your life in me.

Help me be an example of your teachings and your Law, efface all the negative aspects of my life, and help me always strive for goodness and greatness.

Amen.

---

[9] Ezekiel 34:12 (NJB).
[10] Ezekiel 34:6 (NJB).

A Prayer to Jesus When in Danger

* * * * * *

Jesus! Jesus! Jesus! Help me. I am in danger.
  Amen.

A Prayer to Help Follow God and Resist Temptation

* * * * * *

Lord Jesus, help me follow your Law on every ground that I set my feet upon.

Permit me to be in accord with your Law.

Help me be obedient, levelheaded, and focused in everything I do.

Help me always resist the devil's temptations and stay focused on you—and you alone.

Amen.

A Prayer to Help Love God's Creation

❋ ❋ ❋ ❋ ❋ ❋

Lord Jesus, you have shown me how to love by dying on the cross for me.

Please help me understand the sacrifice you have made in order to save me and others from the deceitful legion that has attracted and destroyed so many lives here on earth.

Help me see your face and your love in everything created by you—and help me love like you.

Amen.

A Prayer to Help Stay in God's Care and Boundaries

* * * * * *

Lord Jesus, "clothe my nakedness"[11] with your finest clothes and help me understand you better.

Help me love my neighbors the same way that I love you.

You are the living God, and you turned water into wine. Turn me into your goodness—and make me a miracle of yours.

Without you, I do not know my way. I am lost. Without you, I have nowhere to turn and have nowhere to go.

Lord of all, save a soul that is in peril and needs your care. Amen.

---

[11] Matthew 25:36 (NABRE).

A Prayer to Help Follow
Our Savior, Jesus

❋ ❋ ❋ ❋ ❋ ❋

Lord Jesus, "you are the way, the truth and the life."[12]

Help me come to know your way.

Help me follow you in everything I do—whether or not I am in church.

Help me follow you and seek your presence anywhere I am and everywhere I go.

Without you, I am in the middle of the ocean—and I do not know how to swim.

Help me follow your lead and love everything good that is around me.

Amen.

---

[12] John 14:6 (NABRE).

A Prayer to Help Stay on Principles and Be in the Lord's Presence

※ ※ ※ ※ ※ ※

Jesus, Jesus, Jesus! "You are the truth."[13] Let me be in that truth.

"You are the way."[14] Let me follow that path.

"You are the life."[15] Let me live in your presence.

You are an Evangelist. Let me be in your light.

You are the living Bread. Feed me each and every day. Amen.

---

[13] John 14:6 (NABRE).
[14] John 14:6 (NABRE).
[15] John 14:6 (NABRE).

A Prayer to Help Imitate Jesus, the Christ

* * * * * *

Lord Jesus Christ, I am on the road, and I don't know where it leads me.

Let the end of it be in your sanctuary.

Let me imitate you on a daily basis and let others see you in me.

Make me clean, pure, and sharp—and make me love everything that is in your loving care.

Help me love everything you have died for.

Amen.

A Prayer to Help See God's Love and Follow God

❀ ❀ ❀ ❀ ❀ ❀

Lord of all, help me always stay true to your Law.

You showed the way to the human race by sacrificing your body and saving the world.

"You made the blind man see,"[16] "you raised the dead,"[17] "you turned water into wine,"[18] and "you made five loaves of bread and two fish fed more than five thousand guests."[19]

Help us see you in us—and help us follow your footsteps so that one day we can sing joyfully with your Angels and Saints in heaven.

Amen.

---

[16] John 9:1–12 (NJB).
[17] John 11:1–44 (NJB).
[18] John 2:1–11 (NJB).
[19] Matthew 14:13–21 (NJB).

A Prayer to Help Be an Example of God's Grace

Dear Jesus, let your life flourish in my life so I can be like you.

Keep me under your care always—and let your love flow into my heart.

Help me be the person who you want me to be—and make me tractable to your Law.

Help me be a paragon to our society here on earth in order to strengthen your Kingdom.

Amen.

A Prayer to Our Lord
to Keep Safe

* * * * * *

Lord of all, when my world is upside down, you bring me to life.

Help me help rescind the restless violence that is going on in this world today.

Help me protect your children who are subject to violence, prejudice, injustice, and discrimination today.

Help me find a safe place for them to "take refuge"[20] and help them live in a more peaceful world.

Amen.

---

[20] Psalm 57:1 (NJB).

A Prayer to Stay Clean and Stay in God's Spirit

* * * * * *

Lord Jesus, let me be at peace if I am meant to be monetarily poor though spiritually rich.

Help me stay away from anything unclean and impure.

Help me see no value in vanities—instead see the abundance of your love and your Law.

Help me bear insults.

Let me be steadfast and attentive in everything you have provided for me to learn.

Help me defend your love in every place and everywhere I step.

Let me be gracious for everything you have done for me.

Help me carry the same unconditional love for others that you have for me.

Amen.

A Prayer to Help Live in the Lord's Spirit

✼ ✼ ✼ ✼ ✼ ✼

Lord Jesus, help me know nothing but you, your truth, and your people.

Help me love nothing but you and your children, and see nothing but good for myself and my neighbors.

Help me live in your Spirit and never engage in sophistry, immorality, or dubious claims.

Help me always follow your guidance.

Help me understand the nature of your mission, and be in your presence at all times.

Amen.

A Prayer to Help Resist Temptation

＊ ＊ ＊ ＊ ＊ ＊

Dear Jesus, help me quell any temptation that may sway my way.

Help me rescind any dubious thinking and understand your plan for me.

Elevate my mind to a different level, make it sharp, and help me always take the right approach to everything I come across or come in contact with.

Help me be prudent and vigilant so that I can always see your Law and be able to distinguish between good and evil.

Help me always think like you, breathe like you, and understand your vision and the plans you have for me on earth and in heaven.

Amen.

A Prayer to Help follow God's lead

* * * * * *

Lord of all, "keep me under the shadow of Your wings."[21]

Help me to have always your Spirit in me, love my neighbors like I love you, never criticize my brothers and sisters, and always stay calm in every situation.

Help me never to get worried and know you are here for me and will protect me.

Help me never to get sporadic or erratic around your living creatures.

Help me to follow always your lead and your command, keep your Spirit in my heart, and always see you in everything.

Amen.

---

[21] Psalm 91:4 (NJB).

A Prayer to Help Live in Accordance with God's Law

* * * * * *

Lord Jesus, help us live in accordance with your Law in our communities.

"Let Your river of peace flow"[22] in us so that we can always do what is right and acceptable to you. Help us breathe peace and taste and cherish the love you have given to every citizen in our communities.

Help us to stay wise and levelheaded so that we can always remain within in the boundaries of your Law.

Let your eyes be our light—and let your love be our safety.

Never let us fall into darkness and protect us at all times.

Amen.

---

[22] Isaiah 66:12 (DRA).

A Prayer to Help Love Others Like God

* * * * * *

Dear Lord, without you in my life, I would not know what to do.

Without you, my life would be obsolete.

Without you, my life would be empty.

Help me always love my brothers and sisters and remain in you at all times.

Help me always see you in them and love them like I love you.

Amen.

Section III
PRAYERS TO THE BLESSED MOTHER AND ST. JOSEPH

A Prayer to Help Follow God's Example

* * * * * *

Hail Mary! Mother of God, you are the Model that we should follow.

You have the perfect love that we should cherish in our hearts.

You are the Mother who never wavers and never stops loving her children.

Help us follow your example and always love God, ourselves, and everything that is attributed to God and his Kingdom.

Amen.

A Prayer to the Holy Mother of God to Help Stay in God's Presence

* * * * * *

"Hail Mary, Mother of God,"[23] embrace me under your loving care.

Help me have a heart of love so that I can love God with all my heart.

Help me keep that flame of God's love inside me.

Help me stay in the circumference of God's love, always love others, and carry your example wherever I am.

Amen.

---

[23] Luke 1:28–32 (NABRE).

A Prayer to Help Make the Right Decisions and Stay in Harmony with God

❀ ❀ ❀ ❀ ❀ ❀

Hail Holy Mother of God, your cooperation with God helps bring deliverance to the world.

Help us cooperate with the Law of God and his precepts.

Help us make judicious decisions and work in harmony with our Lord so that one day we can sing and praise Him for all eternity.

Amen.

A Prayer to Help be obedient to God's Law

* * * * * *

Dear Mother, Queen of the universe, you showed obedience to God by helping bring his Son into this world.

Please! Help us to be obedient to your Son, our Lord Jesus Christ, so that we can follow his example wherever we go.

Help us to mold our thinking and our actions into his so that we may follow his image wherever we go.

Help us carry his cross so that we may be united with Him one day for all eternity.

Amen.

A Prayer to Help Stay Focused on our Obligation and Help Protect Our Loved Ones

* * * * * *

Dear Mother, your love for your children is incomparable.

You showed every mother how to love her children by giving care to your Son, our Lord, Jesus Christ.

Show us how to care for our loved ones and show us how to love and protect our children on a daily basis.

Give us the strength to continue the journey of motherhood that we are embarking upon.

Help us strive for greatness and share the love that you give us as your children—and help us pass it to our children.

Help us stay focused and aware of how to fulfill our everyday obligations.

Amen.

A Prayer to Help Come Back to the Father, Your God, and Help Find the Way

❋ ❋ ❋ ❋ ❋ ❋

O blessed ever Virgin, you have unconditional love for your children and always protect them.

Please help us to protect those who do not know God's way yet—and help them come to grips and better understand God's Law.

Help them find their way back to their "Father's house."[24]

Help brighten their minds and soften their hearts so that they can come to know the truth and the living Law that God has created for us.

Amen.

---

[24] John 14:2 (NABRE).

A Prayer to Help Stay under the Blessed Mother's Care

Dear Mother, protect us as your children in this community and keep us safe.

Help us to live always in tranquility as a community and as a family.

You are the Mother of all. You are always loving and taking care of Your children—please gather us under your wings of safety.

Keep us under your protection and lead us under the Spirit of your Son, our Lord, Jesus Christ.

Help us to stay always in Christ's presence—now and forever.

Amen.

A Prayer to Help Foster Those Who Are under God's Care and Love

* * * * * *

Dear St. Joseph, as you fostered the child Jesus, our Savior, under your care, help foster those who are under God's care and God's love.

Help us do the same for our children; they are deeply in need of love and care.

Help us be models in our children's and in our families lives.

Revitalize our spirits and help us stay in God's Spirit.

Help us do what is acceptable to God and "carry the image of God" wherever we go.

Amen.

A Prayer to St. Joseph to Help Always Show God's Love to Your Spouse

※ ※ ※ ※ ※ ※

O St. Joseph my foster father, you accepted Mary as your spouse—even when you were facing difficulties.

Please help me always respect my spouse—even when we are facing difficulties. Help me follow your example and stay firm in our commitments to our loved ones.

Help me bear insults—even when I am right.

Help me be devoted and dedicate my life to my spouse and those who are around me and under my care.

Amen.

Section IV
PRAYERS TO THE HOLY SPIRIT AND THE HOLY ANGELS

A Prayer to Help Walk with God and Proclaim His Love to His Children

* * * * * *

Spirit of heavenly God, help strengthen my heart, mind, and soul to carry the cross of our Lord, Jesus Christ, with love, care, and tenderness.

Help me always do what is acceptable to God with prudence and guidance.

Help me teach the truth and nothing but the truth.

Help me embrace your Laws and precepts with joy.

Help me serve you with love and happiness, see others before myself, and be in your presence always.

Help me proclaim God's Gospel to his children with passion, peace, and joy wherever I may go.

Help me be "the salt of the earth and light of the world" in everything I do.

Help me be at God's side always.

Amen.

A Prayer to Help Protect You from Danger

* * * * * *

Holy Spirit, protect me from any danger that may come my way.

Help me see my enemy's intentions beforehand.

Make me invisible to their eyes and "be my fortress, my refuge, my rock, my shield, my saving strength, my stronghold, and my safety net."

"Save me from violence" and any malicious intent that may come my way.

Be by safety net always.

Amen.

A Prayer to Help Protect Children from Abuse

* * * * * *

Holy Spirit of the Most High, help protect God's children from abuse by others.

Help protect them from predators and any malicious intent that may come their way.

Walk with them at all times and protect them from any danger.

Help rescind and debunk any acts against God's children.

Help local authorities discover and find any potential dangers that may come their way.

Amen.

A Prayer to Help You Be in God's Presence

* * * * * *

Holy Spirit, be in my mind so I can think like God.

Be in my vision so I can see like God.

Be my voice and strength so I can help facilitate God's mission in a more beautiful way.

Be in my heart and soul so others may see the love, the light, and the Spirit of the living God through me.

Help me embrace God's Laws and precepts in everything I do.

Amen.

A Prayer to the Holy Angels to Keep Safe from Danger

O Holy Angels of God, Cherubim and Seraphim with the power of God, protect me always.

Keep me at God's side all day long.

Help me be prudent in my everyday activities, keep me safe at all times, and protect me from danger.

Amen.

A Prayer to Stay Steadfast Against the Enemy of God

* * * * * *

St. Michael the Archangel, your name means "Who is like God."[25]

Help the children of God always resist the temptations of the devil. Protect them from all arms, impure spirits, deceitful tongues, and minds that seek to destroy their souls and the entire human race.

Help the children stay steadfast against the enemy of God and focused on God's missions throughout the world.

Amen.

---

[25] 1 Thessalonians 4:16 (NJB).

A Prayer to Help Keep You Safe

✳ ✳ ✳ ✳ ✳ ✳

Angel of God, keep me safe always.

Protect me from all evil and be at my side both day and night.

Spread your wings over the areas I travel so I can be safe.

Pave the roads for me and make them clean and easy for me to travel.

Assist me in all my needs and protect me always from all the dangers so that I can continue to "proclaim the words of my Lord,"[26] Jesus Christ.

Amen.

---

[26] Mark 16:15 (NJB).

Section V
PRAYERS FOR SPECIAL OCCASIONS AND INTENTIONS

A Prayer for Success
on Your Exams

* * * * * *

Lord Jesus, as I am about to take this exam, open my brain and help me decipher and remember everything I have learned in this class from the beginning until now.

Make my mind "sharp like two-edged swords."[27] and help me go through this exam like drinking water.

Help me stay focused, give my best effort, and pass it with ease.

Amen.

---

[27] Hebrews 4:12 (NJB).

A Prayer to Help Prepare to Meet God in the Next Life

* * * * * *

Lord of Hosts, today—as I am about to leave this world—I leave my life in your hands.

Carry me in your arms like your Mother carried you in her arms as a child.

Purify my soul and help me be your servant forever.

Help me be a part of your choir and your company.

Open the gates of heaven for me and make me one your Saints.

"Help me reach the path of salvation and lead me to Your Kingdom."[28]

Amen.

---

[28] Luke 3:4–6 (NJB).

A Prayer to God to Help Proclaim the Good News

❋ ❋ ❋ ❋ ❋ ❋

Lord Jesus, you were—and are—an itinerant Preacher, Rabbi, Leader, and our Lord.

Help us always see you and your perfections around the globe.

Help us serve you always in a manner that is acceptable to you.

Help us find a deep understanding of your Laws and always live in your presence.

Help us follow your path as a preacher and leader.

Give us the power "to proclaim Your Gospel"[29] and open the eyes of those who cannot see your Laws and your wonders.

Amen.

---

[29] Matthew 24:14 (NABRE).

A Prayer for Special Intentions

❀ ❀ ❀ ❀ ❀ ❀

Eternal Father, you have the eyes to see everything that is clean and unclean, pure and impure.

You are the panacea for every problem that exists.

Help me overcome all the difficulties I am facing today.

Help me see your light and keep me close to you at all times.

Amen.

A Prayer before Receiving Holy Communion

* * * * * *

Dear God, as I am about to receive your Holy Communion at this moment, make my body, my mind, and my soul into yours.

Turn me into your body, cleanse me, and purify my soul and every single cell of my body with your blood.

Make me one with your Spirit and your Laws.

May your Bread of life help me stay and live in your presence from now until eternity.

Amen.

MIKINSON HENRY

A Prayer to Help Carry Out God's Mission

* * * * * *

O blessed St. John the Apostle, please help this community always to stay in God's presence, see God's vision, and give the poor the attention they need.

Ask God to give us strength always, encouragement, and the willingness to carry out his mission and facilitate his plan in our communities.

Amen.

A Prayer to Keep Safe from Injury while Playing Sports

* * * * * *

Heavenly Father, as we begin to play this game, help us stay in your Spirit always.

Help us play the game fair and never insult one another.

Keep us safe from injury and harm—and help us show excellent sportsmanship.

Help us respect ourselves, others, and the game we play.

Through Christ, our Lord.

Amen.

A Prayer before or during Surgery

* * * * * *

Dear Lord, as the doctors begin this surgery, help them stay focused on their task and lead them and guide them so they can make the best decisions.

Help them always make prudent decisions for their patients and keep them in your presence always.

Help them stay focused on their responsibilities so they can perform their task perfectly.

Amen.

Section VI
PRAYERS FOR PROTECTION

A Prayer to Overcome Evil

No evil can come near your tent,
Give yourself to God, and you will be safe,
O my Jesus, St. Michael the Archangel, hail, holy Queen.

No malice can come near your bed,
Give yourself to God, and you will be safe,
O my Jesus, St. Michael the Archangel, hail, holy Queen.

No harsh words can penetrate your lips,
Give yourself to God, and you will be safe,
O my Jesus, St. Michael the Archangel, hail, holy Queen.

No avarice or vanity can take over your life,
Give yourself to God, and you will be safe,
O my Jesus, St. Michael the Archangel, hail, holy Queen.

You will not be a slave of the devil; instead, you will be in
God's hands.
Give yourself to God, and you will be safe,
O my Jesus, St. Michael the Archangel, hail, holy Queen.

God will never let you down; he will protect from unclean spirits.
Give yourself to God, and you will be safe,
O my Jesus, St. Michael the Archangel, hail, holy Queen.

You will be the observer of God's Law forever,
Give yourself to God, and you will be safe,
O my Jesus, St. Michael the Archangel, hail, holy Queen.
Amen.

A Prayer to Help protect from evil doers

* * * * * *

Eternal Father, take me in your loving arms and protect me from all evil intent that may come my way.

Let nothing that is unclean, impure, or unwise come between me and you.

"Mold me into your love, because you are my Father; I am the clay, and you my potter; and all I am the work of your hand."[30]

Keep me in your presence and in your safety net.

Make me invisible in the eyes of the evildoers and let me stay in your presence forever.

Amen.

---

[30] Isaiah 64:7 (NABRE).

A Prayer for God's Protection

* * * * * *

Dear God, protect your children who are being persecuted.

Protect those who are under your care. Shield them from any attack that is coming their way.

Make them invisible and impervious to the malice of evildoers.

Help your children come to understand your Laws and your precepts so they can behave in a manner that accords with your Laws.

Help them to come to grips with the fact that your Laws turn water into wine and give wings to those who follow them.

Help them know that you are the only God that exists.

"Mold them"[31] into your Spirit, help them have clean hearts, and help them understand what is acceptable to you.

Amen.

---

[31] Isaiah 64:7 (NJB).

A Prayer for Protection and to Always Do What Is Pleasing to God

* * * * * *

Dear Father, protect us always. As we begin this journey, help us always do what is pleasing to you and our neighbors.

Help us engage in activities that can lead us to your Kingdom.

"Make our paths straight"[32] and clear, pave the road for us, and keep it safe and sound so that one day we can sing and praise you with all your Angels and Saints in heaven.

Amen.

---

[32] Proverbs 3:6 (NABRE).

A Prayer to Help Keep Communities Safe

* * * * * *

Almighty God, today we come to you as a community and ask you to always keep your eyes on us.

Keep us safe and sound each and every day.

Help us live in harmony, share your love with people in our community, respect the opinions of others, and always stay true to your Laws and precepts.

Amen.

A Prayer to Help Protect
Mothers and Unborn Babies

* * * * * *

Lord of Hosts, protect mothers and unborn babies.

Grant them an easy path to delivery—and keep them safe under your care.

Be the light for them and always keep them under your safety net.

Give them the strength and courage to carry through—even when their journeys seem to be long.

Always give them joy and happiness so they can take care of their loved ones.

Amen.

A Prayer for the Protection of Teachers and Evangelizers

❋ ❋ ❋ ❋ ❋ ❋

Dear loving God, protect teachers and evangelizers.

Help them always lead their students and your people in the right direction.

Help them give the right teachings to your children and do everything according to your Laws.

Help them see the importance of teaching your words.

Enlighten them and others so that they may never get jaded about sharing your essential teachings and lessons with others.

"Mold them into the spirit of your teachings and make them like you."[33]

Amen.

---

[33] Isaiah 64:7 (NJB).

A Prayer of Protection for Those Who Need Help

* * * * * *

Dear Jesus, protect those who have nowhere to go, to sleep, or to eat.

Help them find a solution for their problems.

Provide them with shelter, food, clothes, and drink.

Help them stay in good spirits, mentally and physically, so they do not lose hope.

Turn their misery into greatness.

Keep them always under the safety net of your umbrella and give them your living water so they will never be thirsty again.

Amen.

A Prayer for the Protection of the Pope

* * * * * *

Almighty Father, protect the pope—the successor of St. Peter—help him to make always the right decision, and give him the strength to carry on the journey.

Transform him into a rock like Peter—and help him guide and lead your people in the right direction.

May he always have the right approach for your church and the people—whoever he is shepherding.

Amen.

A Prayer to God the Father for Protection

＊ ＊ ＊ ＊ ＊ ＊

Dear Father, protect me! "Keep me under the shadow of your wing."[34]

Protect me from vicious enemies.

Let your angels shield me from any malicious intent.

Keep me under your rest—and help me see the light that you have created for me.

Protect me from falling into darkness, "mold me into one of your own,"[35] and make me your child again.

Amen.

---

[34] Psalm 17:8–9 (NABRE).

[35] Isaiah 64:7 (NJB).

A Prayer to Help Protect Children from Danger

* * * * * *

Dear God, always protect your children.

Let no evil come near them.

Spare them from every trouble and danger. Save them from getting trapped by evil spirits.

Help those who come to your church to always carry your image inside and outside the church.

Help them always stay in your presence wherever they go.

Transform them into the greatness and the likeness of your handmaid.

Amen.

A Prayer to Help Protect God's Children

* * * * * *

Mother of mercy, help protect your children who are suffering and struggling every single day.

Help them find solutions to their problems.

Help them see the light that seems so far away.

Help them never be discouraged—no matter what their situation is.

Help them keep their "faith, hope, and love"[36] alive in order to meet their Savior one day.

Amen.

---

[36] 1 Corinthians 13:13 (NABRE).

A Prayer to Protect
All Mothers

✦ ✦ ✦ ✦ ✦ ✦

Dear Mother, your love is so real!

I was a lost child, and you embraced me with Your loving care.

Please keep all mothers under your care and your Spirit—and help them see the light that you are showing them each and every day.

Help them to follow your example and strive for greatness and to be role models like you.

Make them your children forever.

Amen.

A Prayer to Help Protect the Authorities in a Country

* * * * * *

Dear God, protect the authorities in this country.

Help them see and fight for the interests of their own people and for those who cannot help themselves.

Open their eyes so they can see more clearly.

Help them make the right decisions and always work for the unity and best interests of this great nation.

Amen.

A Prayer for Protection against Evil

* * * * * *

St. Michael, St. Gabriel, and St. Raphael, protect the little children of God from predators and any malicious intent that might come their way.

Let no evil come their way—and protect them at all times from those who do evil.

Assist them in their special needs, hide them under the shadow of God's Wings, and continually keep them safe.

Amen.

A Prayer for God's protection while asleep

✻ ✻ ✻ ✻ ✻ ✻

Dear God, bedtime is near. Protect me in my sleep.
Let my night be tranquil.
Let your Angels surround me through the night.
Let my night be in your hands and at your rest.
Amen.

A Prayer to Help Protect the Vulnerable and Stay Committed to Help Facilitate God's Work and Mission

* * * * * *

Loving God, help us remember those who give their lives for the safety of your children and others.

Give them the strength and courage to continue the journeys they are taking to strengthen your Kingdom.

Help them always protect those who are under their care and fight the clouds of injustice that seem to occupy the whole world.

Help them avoid becoming lethargic in their commitments to do your work around the globe.

Amen.

A Prayer to Help Protect against Evildoers

❋ ❋ ❋ ❋ ❋ ❋

Dear God, you have created me to be your child—please help me not fall into the side of darkness.

Illuminate my soul like a candle that is never extinguished.

"You have created the heavens,"[37] and it belongs to you. Please help me see your wonders and respect your Laws.

"You have created the earth with all its creatures,"[38] and they also belong to you. Help me always stay in the light of your presence.

Protect me as your child, help me never surrender to evildoers, and make me firm like a rock.

Amen.

---

[37] Genesis 1:1 (NABRE).
[38] Genesis 1:1, 21 (NABRE).

A Prayer for God's Protection

* * * * * *

Dear Father, protect me always.

Let your temple be my light and my direction when I do not know where to go.

Cleanse my desiccated mind—and let me see your love for me.

Let me run to you at all times—whether I am in trouble or not.

Change my heart to be more like yours and make me your child again.

Amen.

A Protection Prayer for Those Who Are Ministering Your Church

* * * * * *

God of gods, Lord of lords, protect those who are ministering your church.

Help them not fall into darkness and always give them strength so they can continue to do the wonderful jobs they are doing around the world.

Never let them get lethargic about teaching, preaching, evangelizing, or raising the spirits of those who are in need and under your care.

Always help them focus on the missions that they have been given by you, always help them see the priority of your missions throughout the world, and help them be strong like a rock.

Amen.

A Prayer for the Protection of Schoolchildren

* * * * * *

Dear God, always protect schoolchildren.

Keep them from any danger and abnormal activities that may come their way.

Keep them always under your protection and your power.

Help them keep their eyes open, stay vigilant, and stay away from malicious minds and deceitful tongues that can affect their well-being.

Amen.

A Prayer for Protection to Those Who Have Trust in the Lord

✴ ✴ ✴ ✴ ✴ ✴

In the name of the Father, and of the Son, and of the Holy Spirit:

Blessed are they who put their trust in God.
The Lord will never leave them in shambles,
Our Father, hail Mary, glory be.

Blessed are they who put their trust in God.
He will save them from the mouth of the beast.
Our Father, hail Mary, glory be.

Blessed are they who put their trust in God.
He will keep them away from any malicious mind at a distance.
Our Father, hail Mary, glory be.

Blessed are they who put their trust in God.
He will save his children from the attacks that corrupt minds are plotting against them.
Our Father, hail Mary, glory be.

Blessed are they who put their trust in God.
He will keep them new like the morning dew.
Our Father, hail Mary, glory be.

Blessed are they who put their trust in God.
They are not afraid of anything as long as they keep his Law
in their hearts.
Our Father, hail Mary, glory be.

Blessed are they who put their trust in God.
Under the shadow of his wings, their souls will rest.
Our Father, hail Mary, glory be.

Blessed are they who put their trust in God.
He will save them from this hostile environment and keep
them at peace.
Our Father, hail Mary, glory be.

Blessed are they who put their trust in God.
They will be as tall the sky, as bright as the stars, as big as
the universe, and as wise as the spirit. They will be in state of
grace, and they will be temples of the Holy Spirit.
Our Father, hail Mary, glory be.

Blessed are they who put their trust in God.
He will never let them down, and they will be his children
forever.
Our Father, hail Mary, glory be.

Blessed are they who put their trust in God.
His army will keep them safe, and not a hair will come out of
their skin.
Our Father, hail Mary, glory be.

Blessed are they who put their trust in God.
He will be their light when darkness comes and their strength
when weakness is at their doorstep.
Our Father, hail Mary, glory be.

Blessed are they who put their trust in God.
Night will be their morning, and morning will be their
sunlight.
Our Father, hail Mary, glory be.

Blessed are they who put their trust in God.
They will keep their eyes open, following the vision of God in
their hearts, minds, and souls.
Our Father, hail Mary, glory be.

Blessed are they who put their trust in God.
He will be with them day and night—and never let unclean
spirits violate them.
Our Father, hail Mary, glory be.

Blessed are they who put their trust in God.
He will be their lion, and they will be his cubs.
Our Father, hail Mary, glory be.

Blessed are they who put their trust in God.
He will spare them from the teeth of ferocious beasts.
Our Father, hail Mary, glory be.

Blessed are they who put their trust in God.
He will protect them and give them strength as long as they
live in his presence.
Our Father, hail Mary, glory be.

Blessed are they who put their trust in God.
He will save them from the fiery lake and keep them from
falling into a hole.
Our Father, hail Mary, glory be.

Blessed are they who put their trust in God.
They will be impervious to danger and to their own
wrongdoing.
Our Father, hail Mary, glory be.

Blessed are they who put their trust in God.
Under his tent is where their lives will be, and under his love
is where their cares will rest.
Our Father, hail Mary, glory be.

Blessed are they who put their trust in God.
For they are his children, and he is their God forever.
Our Father, hail Mary, glory be.

Blessed are they who put their trust in God.
His true love shall be shown to them, and his protection shall
encircle them.
Our Father, hail Mary, glory be.

Blessed are they who put their trust in God.
The wicked will pay a price they cannot bear for attempting
to attack a child of God.
Our Father, hail Mary, glory be.

Blessed are they who put their trust in God.
He will show his children life when death is near.
Our Father, hail Mary, glory be.

Blessed are they who put their trust in God.
He will show them love when hate is around.
Our Father, hail Mary, glory be.

Blessed are they who put their trust in God.
He will let the wicked know that He is the God of all.
Our Father, hail Mary, glory be.

Blessed are they who put their trust in God.
He will revitalize their spirits and make them fountains of joy
in which life is alive.
Our Father, hail Mary, glory be.

Blessed are they who put their trust in God.
With him, there is no darkness; there is only light.
Our Father, hail Mary, glory be.

Blessed are they who put their trust in God.
Nothing can come between them and their God.
Our Father, hail Mary, glory be.

Blessed are they who put their trust in God.
No evil can penetrate a heart that is in God and in God alone.
Our Father, hail Mary, glory be.

Blessed are they who put their trust in God.
He will help them in their tribulation, and He will save their
capsizing world.
Our Father, hail Mary, glory be.

Blessed are they who put their trust in God.

He will hide them in his tabernacle, and they will be invisible in the eyes of evildoers.

Our Father, hail Mary, glory be.

With the protection of the Lord, no evil can come near me:

By the sacrificial blood of our Lord and the Lamb that was slain, I will be safe.
By Christ's death and resurrection, I will be safe.
By abiding by his Law, I will be safe.
By his miracles on hearth and heaven, I will be safe.
By the protection of his noble army, I will be safe.
By his angels and martyrs, I will be safe.
By his love and care, I will be safe.
By his power and might, I will be safe.

Let us pray:

Lord Jesus, you died on the cross for our salvation. Protect us from the hands of the enemy. Make us solid like a rock and impervious to any malicious intent. Spare us from the jaws of evildoers. Cleanse us from any unclean spirits that want to destroy our lives. Hide us under your wings and rest our souls under the care and the power of your hands.
Amen.

The following prayers and creeds are needed to complete your journey:

- Our Father
- Hail Mary
- Glory Be
- The Nicene Creed
- The Apostle's Creed
- Fatima Prayer
- Hail, Holy Queen
- Michael the Archangel

The Our Father

Our Father, who art in heaven, hallowed be thy name; thy
Kingdom come, thy will be done on earth as it is in heaven.
Give us this day our daily bread, and forgive us our trespasses
as we forgive those who trespass against us, and lead us not
into temptation, but deliver us from evil.
Amen.

Hail Mary

Hail Mary, full of Grace, the Lord is with thee.
Blessed are thou amongst women and blessed is the fruit of
thy womb, Jesus.
Holy Mary Mother of God,
pray for us sinners now and at the hour of our death.
Amen.

Glory Be

Glory be to the Father and to the Son and to the Holy Spirit.
As it was in the beginning is now, and ever shall be, world
without end.
Amen.

The Nicene Creed

We believe in one God,
the Father, the Almighty,
Maker of all that is, seen and unseen.
We believe in one Lord, Jesus Christ,
the only Son of God,
eternally begotten of the Father,
God from God, Light from Light,
true God from true God,
begotten, not made, consubstantial
of one Being with the Father.
Through him, all things were made.
For us men and for our salvation
he came down from heaven,
and by the Holy Spirit was incarnate of the Virgin Mary,
and became man.
For our sake, he was crucified under Pontius Pilate;
he suffered death and was buried.
On the third day he rose again
in accordance with the scriptures;
he ascended into heaven
and is seated at the right hand of the Father.
He will come again in glory to judge the living and the dead,
and his kingdom will have no end.
We believe in the Holy Spirit, the Lord, the giver of life,
who proceeds from the Father and the Son.
With the Father and the Son, he is worshipped and glorified.
He has spoken through the prophets.
We believe in one holy Catholic and apostolic Church.
We acknowledge one baptism for the forgiveness of sins.
We look for the resurrection of the dead,
and the life of the world to come.
Amen.

The Apostle's Creed

I believe in God,
the Father Almighty,
Creator of heaven and earth,
and in Jesus Christ, his only Son, our Lord,
who was conceived by the Holy Spirit,
born of the Virgin Mary,
suffered under Pontius Pilate,
was crucified, died, and was buried.
He descended into hell;
on the third day, he rose again from the dead.
He ascended into heaven,
and is seated at the right hand of God, the Father Almighty.
From there, he will come to judge the living and the dead.
I believe in the Holy Spirit,
the Holy Catholic Church,
the communion of saints,
the forgiveness of sins,
the resurrection of the body,
and life everlasting.
Amen.

Fatima Prayer

O my Jesus, forgive us our sins, save us from the fires of hell and lead all souls to heaven, especially those who are in most need of thy mercy.

Hail, Holy Queen Prayer

Hail, holy Queen,
Mother of mercy,
our life, our sweetness, and our hope.
To thee do we cry,
poor banished children of Eve:
to thee do we send up our sighs,
mourning and weeping in this valley of tears.
Turn then, most gracious advocate,
thine eyes of mercy toward us,
and after this our exile,
show unto us the blessed fruit of thy womb, Jesus,
O clement, O loving,
O sweet Virgin Mary!
Amen.

Prayer to Holy Michael
the Archangel

* * * * * *

Holy Michael, the Archangel, defend us in battle. Be our safeguard against the wickedness and snares of the devil. May God rebuke him, we humbly pray; and do you, O Prince of the heavenly host, by the power of God cast into hell Satan and all the evil spirits who wander through the world seeking the ruin of souls.

Amen.

Sources

* * * * * *

Scripture quotations marked NABRE are from The New
American Bible, Revised Edition.
Copyright 1986, 2011, by USCCB. Used by permission. All
right reserved Worldwide.

Scripture quotations marked DRBO are from Douay-Rheims
Bible, copyright DRBO.ORG
2001–2017. All rights reserved.
Scripture quotations marked NJB are from The New Jerusalem
Bible, copyright© 1985 by Darton, Longman & Todd, Ltd. and
Doubleday, a division of Random House, Inc. Reprinted by
Permission.

Shutterstock.com

Printed in the United States
by Baker & Taylor Publisher Services